THE LIBRARY OF
HIP-HOP
BIOGRAPHIES™

Missy Elliott

Bethany Bezdecheck

ROSEN
PUBLISHING

New York

Dedicated to Class 619 at P.S. 327

Published in 2009 by The Rosen Publishing Group, Inc.
29 East 21st Street, New York, NY 10010

Library of Congress Cataloging-in-Publication Data

Bezdecheck, Bethany.
Missy Elliott. — 1st ed.
    p. cm. — (The library of hip-hop biographies)
Includes bibliographical references and index.
ISBN-13: 978-1-4358-5056-9 (library binding)
ISBN-13: 978-1-4358-5442-0 (pbk)
ISBN-13: 978-1-4358-5448-2 (6 pack)
1. Elliott, Missy—Juvenile literature. 2. Singers—United States—Biography—Juvenile literature. 3. Rap musicians—United States—Biography—Juvenile literature. I. Title.
ML3930.E45B49 2009
782.421649092—dc22

[B]

2008019948

Manufactured in the United States of America

On the cover: Missy Elliott attends the first annual Celebrity Hair Show and Beauty Expo in New York in 2007.

CONTENTS

INTRODUCTION

She may be just five feet two inches tall, but Missy "Misdemeanor" Elliott is, without a doubt, one of the most powerful women in hip-hop. Not only is she a superstar rapper, but she is also a successful singer, songwriter, record producer, clothing designer, and charity spokesperson. She has won four Grammy Awards and is the only female rapper to have six platinum albums.

Growing up, Elliott simply knew that she would become a star. Not everyone agreed with her. People reminded her that star musicians lived in mansions in New York or Los Angeles. Elliott was living in a trailer park in Virginia. The famous women that she and her friends watched on television were tall and thin. Elliott was short and overweight. But she wouldn't let anyone tell her that she couldn't make it in the music business. She felt that all success really took was talent, motivation, and bravery. She eventually proved herself right.

Elliott has never been afraid to be different, and it is this bravery that has made her so famous. She makes trends instead of following them. Each song she creates is unlike anything fans have ever heard before. Therefore, no one can ever wait to see what exciting tracks she will lay down next!

Missy Elliott is also unique because she is one of the few female record producers in the world. As a music executive, she has found that men don't always take her seriously. She, therefore, has become an outspoken supporter of women's rights, and she works hard to assure women that they can be just as powerful as men. Today, most men in hip-hop wish they could be half as successful as she is!

Although Elliott has already accomplished more than most could accomplish in ten lifetimes, her career is still going strong. This is good news for hip-hop fans, who can look forward to hearing even more from this innovative artist.

CHAPTER ONE
MELISSA'S WORLD

"I always created a world . . . [Still] now to this day . . . wherever I want to go in my mind, that's where I want to take the world."
—*Missy Elliott, as spoken during VH1's Hip Hop Honors*

It was inevitable that the great **Missy Elliott**, born Melissa Annette Elliott on July 1, 1971, would one day become a famous musician. By the time she was four years old, she was accustomed to answering "Superstar!" whenever she was asked what she wanted to be when she grew up. Elliott was raised in poverty in Portsmouth, Virginia. She was far from the neon lights of Broadway or the star-paved streets of Hollywood. However, her natural confidence, drive, and enthusiasm made her dreams of stardom achievable.

As a little girl, Elliott enjoyed nothing more than making up and performing songs. She sang about cockroaches, butterflies, passing cars, or whatever happened to be around! She sang to people on the street while standing on overturned trash

DJs use turntables to match the tempos of two different tracks. They experiment to achieve different sounds and beats.

cans. She sang to rows of dolls while locked away in her room.

In the 1970s, the decade of her childhood, hip-hop was just beginning to come to life. DJs in New York City spinning funk and soul music at parties were starting to experiment with the tracks that they were playing. They began to separate the beats from the tracks, creating an exciting new sound that quickly spread throughout the nation. Early MCs such as the legendary DJ Herc later added words to the beats, creating the very first rap songs.

Hip-hop was further developed when DJs began remixing their hits. These popular remixes were made by using new-wave techniques such as scratching and mixing. Scratching, which was performed by moving a vinyl record back and forth on a turntable, produced a distinct, funky sound. Mixing, on the other hand, was the act of combining two different songs to create a brand new track.

Soon after hip-hop was born, rhythm and blues, or R & B, began to enter a major renaissance. R & B is a musical genre that originated in the 1940s. Its renewed popularity was due to the crowd-pleasing hits of new artists including Michael Jackson, Prince, and Whitney Houston. R & B had, by this time, been playing on the radio for decades. However, the influences of funk, soul, and now hip-hop were suddenly giving the genre a new attitude. Its sound was no longer slow and sad. Modern R & B songs were highly danceable, with dramatic, gospel-inspired vocals. It was this contemporary R & B that Elliott loved best. As a student at Manor High School (now Woodrow Wilson High School) in Portsmouth, Virginia, her favorite artists were Michael and Janet Jackson.

GREAT INFLUENCES

Elliott took up writing letters to both Michael and Janet Jackson nearly every day, begging them to come and get her out of class. Figuring that they would help her sign a record deal once they witnessed her talent, Elliott even sent them her class schedule so that they would know where to find her.

Janet Jackson never responded to a single letter that Elliott wrote to her in high school. However, around the year 2000, Jackson did call her to tell her that she loved her music! She asked Elliott to work with her on a remix of her song "Son of a Gun." Elliott wrote and rapped for the remix. She was also in the video, as was Sean "Puff Daddy" Combs.

Not only is Michael Jackson a great musician, he is also a great dancer! His unique style continues to influence dance today and modern artists like Missy Elliott.

MAKING HER MUSIC

Not only was Missy Elliott's active imagination a tool for plotting her path to stardom, it was also a means of survival. Her father, a U.S. marine, would often abuse her mother, giving her cause to retreat into an imaginary world free from her parents' ceaseless fighting. When Elliott turned fourteen years old, she and her mother finally escaped the trailer home that they lived in, leaving Elliott's father and their violent past behind them.

As an only child, Elliott had no brothers or sisters to help her through the tough times. Fortunately, she did have plenty of friends to turn to for support. Her contagious sense of humor made her extremely popular at school. At lunch, kids would run to ask her to join their table. They constantly wanted to be by her side, for she could always make them laugh. Her peers' eagerness to be with her helped to keep her strong, for she could never disappoint an audience.

Elliott's mother, Patricia, also helped maintain her daughter's happiness. She knew that her daughter had been through a lot and, therefore, didn't scold her too much about her incessant music making. She barely even complained when Elliott wrote song lyrics all over her bedroom walls!

As crazy as Elliott was about music, she didn't start listening to hip-hop until she was in her late teens. It was while dancing to the beats of DJ Devastator that she first became hooked on hip-hop's sound. A Virginia DJ, Devastator was known for traveling to New York and bringing back the hottest new records. He would play these tunes at house parties or parties in school gyms. At a house party one evening, he caught Elliott's attention when he put on a record by the female rap artist MC Lyte. "This dude is hot!" Elliott exclaimed to her friends, as told in an interview on VH1's *Hip Hop Honors* awards show. When her friends responded that MC Lyte was a woman, she was even more impressed. She began to wonder if one day she, too, could become a great female rap artist.

MC Lyte signed with record label First Priority when she was just a teenager. Two years later, she became the first rapper to perform at Carnegie Hall.

A very religious woman, Patricia refused to allow her daughter to listen to hip-hop records at home. Elliott would, therefore, go to her friends' houses to hear more of her new favorite type of music. Still interested in writing songs, she began to make up her own lyrics to go along with the tracks that she was hearing. Although she was inspired by other artists, Elliott wanted her raps to be different from anything that she or her friends had heard before. However, her lyrics remained rhymes that others could relate to. Most of her raps and songs were about the situations that she or her friends were experiencing at the time.

As she became more involved in the hip-hop scene, Elliott eventually met Virginia rapper Melvin Barcliff, otherwise known as Magoo. It was through Magoo that she met her future big business partner, Timothy Mosley, known today as the famous music producer Timbaland.

Timbaland was solely a DJ going by the name of DJ Timmy Tim when Elliott first met him at his home in Portsmouth. Thinking she would be interested in hearing Timbaland's music, Magoo brought Elliott along one evening while paying his friend a visit. "He had a little Casio and . . . these big hands," she said of Timbaland on *Hip Hop Honors*. "I started singing over sample stuff that he had . . . [From] that day forth, I would go over there every day after school and we would do records."

It was around this time that Elliott and three of her friends from junior high school—La Shawn Shellman, Chonitah Coleman, and Radiah Scott—decided to form a hip-hop group of their own. They named the group Sista and recruited Timbaland to be their producer. With Timbaland's help, Sista began recording demos. When Elliott was twenty years old, Sista eventually caught the attention of star musician and producer DeVante Swing of Jodeci.

Jodeci, an R & B group that originated in North Carolina, consisted of two sets of brothers: Dalvin and Donald "DeVante

Swing" DeGrate, and Cedric and Joel Hailey. The group was a great inspiration to many later R & B artists. Jodeci was mainly known for producing a style of music called New Jack Swing. This sound combined hip-hop beats with soulful, melodic harmonies. DeVante Swing, the leader of Jodeci, was eventually granted his own imprint by his record label, Elektra. He began recruiting vocalists, writers, and producers to join his imprint, which he named Swing Mob. The members of Swing Mob were encouraged

Jodeci's name is a combination of the Hailey brothers' nicknames, Jo-Jo and K-Ci, and the DeGrates' brothers' last name. The members first met each other through their girlfriends.

to behave as a family, and all twenty-two of them lived together in a two-story house in New York City. Many members of Swing Mob were invited to join the group after auditioning for DeVante Swing following his Jodeci concerts. Sista was determined that this would be the way in which they would break into the music business.

After a Jodeci concert in Portsmouth, Missy Elliott and her fellow Sista members tracked down DeVante Swing at his hotel. The girls sang a few original songs a capella, and their style and skill impressed DeVante considerably. He announced to the members of Sista that they were more than welcome to sign with the Swing Mob imprint. Elliott was overjoyed. Her music career had begun!

CHAPTER TWO
HEE HAW GIRL

"They don't even know my name and they'll say,
'Hee Haw girl, do that slide across the floor.'"
—*Missy Elliott, as told to imusic*

After signing with Swing Mob, Missy Elliott couldn't wait to move to New York City. She was more than ready to start her serious music career . . . on one condition: she insisted that her friends Timbaland and Magoo be allowed to join her. After all, Sista would have never succeeded without their help. DeVante

DeVante Swing named Timothy Mosley "Timbaland" after the footwear brand Timberland. At the time, Timberland boots were especially popular in hip-hop fashion.

Swing agreed to Elliott's proposal. Soon, all six friends were working together at the famous Swing Mob house.

In addition to working on Sista's debut album, Elliott and Timbaland helped write Jodeci tracks while they were with Swing Mob. Writing songs for Jodeci obviously took up time that Elliott could have been devoting to her own career. However, she didn't mind doing the group such favors. She had always enjoyed sharing her gift of songwriting with others. To *Interview* journalist Michael Musto she confirmed, "I really enjoy writing and producing music for other artists. Some people save their best songs for their own albums. I'd rather give another artist one of my songs." This generous attitude of hers was certainly unusual within the cutthroat music business. However, it was often Elliott's unusual choices that brought her success. Indeed, her willingness to give unto others won her a great deal of friends and connections within the music industry. She knew that these friends and connections would one day repay her for her kindness.

Although she was now working and living alongside a great deal of other musicians, Elliott managed to remain authentic. She chose not to draw upon popular songs or consider other artists' styles when she was writing. Instead, she would simply close her eyes, listen to the track that was playing, and write based on how the music made her feel. When gangsta rap, a type of hip-hop that glorifies gang culture, first became popular, Elliott chose not to write for the trend. "[When people] see John Doe died on TV . . . they don't want to turn on their radio and hear about you shooting up, you running up in somebody house or you shipping this here, they want something that's [going to] make them happy," she explained to radio DJ Davey D.

After working on so many songs from behind the scenes, Elliott finally hit the airwaves in 1993. She was featured in the song "That's What Little Girls Are Made Of," which she had written for child star Raven Symoné. Listeners could hear Elliott singing during the song's break, the segment of a song during which there is a break from the main vocals, tune, and beat.

Before releasing her debut album, child star Raven Symoné played three-year-old Olivia Kendall on *The Cosby Show*.

During the break, Elliott created a fun character by singing in a Jamaican accent. She played with Rastafarian language and Caribbean beats. Her performance was a great example of her creativity. However, she was not asked to be in the song's video. Instead, a different woman was hired to lip-sync to Elliott's voice. The woman was thinner than she was, and people began to wonder if the video's producers thought Elliott was too heavy to be on camera. If this were true, then she would soon prove these critics wrong. The very next year, Elliott was showcased both vocally and physically in a second music video. Best of all, this video belonged to Sista!

In 1994, Sista's first music video aired on MTV. The video was created for the single "Brand Nu," from the group's first album. This time, the camera closed in on Elliott during almost every other shot, allowing her to prove that not only skinny women could rule the screen. While the video was a real success, the album, *4 All the Sistas Around da World*, was never released. In 1995, the DeGrate and Hailey brothers decided to go their separate ways, causing Swing Mob to collapse.

Forever determined, Elliott and Timbaland decided that the end of Swing Mob would not be the end of their music careers. Instead, it would be the beginning. They began to work together as a songwriting and production team. They planned on producing hip-hop records unlike anything fans had ever heard before.

One way that Elliott and Timbaland hoped to reform hip-hop was by creating tracks from scratch. At the time, most other hip-hop artists were creating tracks around samples, which are segments of prerecorded songs. Samples were most often constructed from breaks. Sometimes, they were repeated over and over, creating what were called loops. Elliott and Timbaland stood out from other hip-hop artists because they used samples less often. They preferred their music to be more original.

Job offers for her and Timbaland came more and more frequently as news of their unique sound spread throughout the music industry. Before long, they had created hits for an impressive list of artists. However, their careers didn't truly skyrocket until they were introduced to Aaliyah.

AALIYAH

Aaliyah was born Aaliyah Dana Haughton. She was an R & B artist who became successful at a very young age. Her uncle,

Aaliyah, Timbaland, and Missy Elliott became close friends after collaborating on Aaliyah's second album. Aaliyah was later featured on the Missy Elliott track "Best Friends."

music producer Barry Hankerson, knew early on that she had a remarkable talent for singing. He encouraged and supported her as she sang in plays, on the TV show *Star Search*, and with legendary R & B artist Gladys Knight in Las Vegas. When Aaliyah was fourteen years old, her uncle introduced her to one of his clients, the R & B star R. Kelly.

R. Kelly recognized Aaliyah's talent right away. In 1994, he produced her debut album, *Age Ain't Nothing but a Number*. The album went platinum, but Aaliyah knew she could do even better.

Aaliyah hired Missy Elliott and Timbaland to write the majority of the songs on her second album. The album, *One in a Million*, was released when Aaliyah was just seventeen years old. Many of the songs on *One in a Million* soared to the top of the R & B charts, causing the album to go double-platinum. The success of the album made Aaliyah hip-hop royalty. Her achievement even inspired movie producers to cast her in two feature films. The music industry was impressed by what Elliott and Timbaland had done for Aaliyah's career. Artists began clamoring to work with them. While this alone was the type of success Elliott had dreamed of, things were about to get even better.

FINDING HER OWN WAY

In 1995, Sean "Puff Daddy" Combs, the famous head of Bad Boy Records, approached Missy Elliott with a request. This time, it was not a behind-the-scenes job. Combs was familiar with Elliott's work as a rapper, as he had helped develop Jodeci while employed with Uptown Records. He liked her interesting, groundbreaking style, and he wondered if she would like to be featured on hip-hop artist Gina Thompson's song "The Things You Do." Of course, Elliott agreed to the job. The song was an instant hit, and listeners began to wonder just who it was rapping during the song's break. They were finally able to put a face to the voice when Elliott was given a role in the song's video. The video was played often on MTV. As a result, viewers began to recognize Elliott on the street. They would run up to her, calling her "Hee Haw Girl," after the unique way in which she mixed laughter into a slide, or series of scaled notes, during her performance.

Combs was so impressed with Elliott's work on "The Things You Do" that he asked her to rap on MC Lyte's hip-hop anthem "Cold Rock a Party." She couldn't believe her good fortune.

In very little time, she had gone from dancing to her hero at a party to dancing with her hero in a music video! "Cold Rock a Party" became a megahit, and once again, hip-hop fans were head over heels in love with Elliott's work. They saw her as an adventurous, risk-taking artist, and they couldn't wait to see what she would do next.

It was becoming apparent to Combs that Missy Elliott had what it took to become a major star in her own right. In 1996, he decided to ask her to sign with Bad Boy Records as a solo artist. At the same time, Sony Records approached her with a potential record deal. Unfortunately, both parties were a bit too late. She had just been offered her own record label by Elektra Entertainment Group! Elliott named the label Goldmind.

CHAPTER THREE
AGAINST THE GRAIN

Missy Elliott's Goldmind label was launched in 1997 with her first album as a solo artist, *Supa Dupa Fly*. Every song on the album was produced by Timbaland, and Elliott would not have had it any other way. She knew that no other music producer could compete with Timbaland's hot, unexpected beats. Friends of hers, like Ginuwine and Aaliyah, sang and rapped on the album. Hip-hop stars Busta Rhymes and Lil' Kim were also featured on various tracks. Elliott had certainly assembled an impressive lineup of artists

Missy Elliott's CD single "The Rain" *(above)* features a sample from 1970s soul musician Ann Peebles's song "I Can't Stand the Rain." Her work has been sampled by many hip-hop groups, including the Wu-Tang Clan.

to assist her with her big debut. As she had predicted, being a good friend had really paid off!

Critics took note of Elliott's remarkable entourage. At the same time, however, they recognized her as a talented artist on her own. Of *Supa Dupa Fly*, *Entertainment Weekly* reported, "Elliott's songwriting resume reads like a who's who of contemporary R & B . . . [On] her solo debut famous friends like Aaliyah repay the debt . . . But Elliott doesn't need help: She's a wickedly innovative singer-rapper."

Elliott's rising fame allowed her to hire the great Harold "Hype" Williams to direct the video for *Supa Dupa Fly*'s first single, "The Rain." The previous year, Williams had won a Billboard Music Video Award for his direction of Busta Rhymes's "Woo Hah" video. Elliott hoped the video for "The Rain" would have similar success.

"The Rain" video was, like most of her creations, far from standard. It opened with Elliott grooving in a space age setting. Her dance moves were short and lurching, making her appear as if she were a puppet on strings. She wore futuristic goggles and a shiny, black inflated suit. Later, she sat on a hill while special effects made her body swivel and morph.

Many viewers were at first confused by the video for "The Rain." They thought the suit Elliott was wearing in the beginning of the video resembled garbage bags. They wondered why anyone would want to dress in such a bizarre outfit. Other female hip-hop artists wore tight-fitting, revealing clothing. People wondered why Elliott didn't do the same. For her, the inflated suit was an important statement. She wanted to show fans that she was more concerned about her music than her body.

Elliott's refreshing originality won *Supa Dupa Fly* massive respect. Critics adored its lighthearted rhymes and playful sounds. While other hip-hop artists were rapping about gang violence, she was rapping about driving to the beach. Her "beep beeps" and "vroooms" made people smile and forget about their troubles. Eventually, the album went platinum. As for Elliott's inflatable suit, it was later boxed up and sent to the

In 1996, Lil' Kim released her solo debut album. She was previously a member of the group Junior M.A.F.I.A.

Rock & Roll Hall of Fame! Once again, her unusual choices proved to be the foundation for her success.

The same year *Supa Dupa Fly* was released, Missy Elliott was invited to participate in a remix of Lil' Kim's song "Not Tonight." The invitation was an honor, as the remix starred only the hottest ladies of hip-hop. In addition to Lil' Kim and Elliott, it featured Da Brat, Queen Latifah, Lisa "Left Eye" Lopes, and Angie Martinez. In the remix's video, Elliott included moves and looks from "The Rain" in her performance, reminding viewers of just who she was. As she rocked back and forth in orange overalls and sunglasses resembling goggles, she seemed to be saying, "Remember me? You're going to be seeing a lot more of this!"

The ladies of the "Not Tonight" remix were asked to perform their song at the 1997 MTV Video Music Awards. The event was to be especially exciting for Elliott. "The Rain" had been nominated for three awards: Best Rap Video, Best

Breakthrough Video, and Best Direction in a Video. The awards show was highly televised, so people of all ages and tastes in music watched it. By the end of the show, even those who were unfamiliar with hip-hop were now familiar with Missy "Misdemeanor" Elliott. When watching the "Not Tonight" performance, viewers especially enjoyed the way in which she entered from the audience. She was dancing and waving with a big grin on her face, wearing a gold lamé suit that only someone with her daring enthusiasm could rock. Her fun, carefree attitude made her a very likable performer.

Even as a successful solo artist, Elliott chose to keep writing and producing songs for others. When UK "girl power" group the Spice Girls became popular, she volunteered to produce Spice Girl Melanie B's solo debut single. The single's title was "I Want You Back." Elliott's contribution to the record was a true example of her generosity. At first, she had wanted to record the song for her own album. However, she later decided to gift it to Melanie B. She made a guest appearance on the catchy track. She also participated in the video. In the video, Elliott and the Spice Girl paid tribute to Melanie B's nickname, "Scary Spice." They were shot in an eerie green light and wore contact lenses that gave their eyes a creepy look. The song ended up topping the UK Singles Chart. Apparently, Elliott still had a knack for spicing up another artist's career.

In 1999, she released her second solo album, *Da Real World*. As usual, she had teamed up with Timbaland on every

GOLDMIND ARTISTS

- Soul Diggaz
- Tweet
- Jessica Betts
- Lil' Brianna
- Nicole Wray
- Mocha

- Gina Thompson
- Danjamowf
- Torry Carter
- Jasmine
- Lil' Mo
- Derek Rhodes

track. The album was even more star-studded than *Supa Dupa Fly*. This did not come as a surprise to the music industry. Everyone in hip-hop now wanted to work with her. This time, the album's featured artists included Redman, Beyoncé Knowles, and Eminem.

At twenty-eight years old, a more mature Elliott was ready to make a real statement with her music. Many of the songs on *Da Real World* confronted sexism. As one of the only female producers in the music business, Elliott faced sexism daily. To Michael Musto of *Interview*, she explained, "Music is a male-dominated field. Women are not always taken as seriously as we should be, so sometimes we have to put our foot down."

Not only did *Da Real World* contain a more serious message, it also had a more serious sound. "[It] all comes off like a

soundtrack for a dark future," read *Rolling Stone*'s review of the album. Of course, as smart businesspeople, Elliott and Timbaland knew that a completely somber album wouldn't sell. They made sure to include lighter, more upbeat tracks as well, like a remix of her hit single "Hot Boyz." Like *Supa Dupa Fly*, *Da Real World* went platinum and was nominated for several MTV Video Music Awards. It was beginning to seem as if every task that Elliott undertook was inevitably met with success!

By 2000, her career was more than well under way. She decided that she could afford to take a break from creating solo albums. Instead, she began searching for other talented musicians to sign to Goldmind. The first artists that she recruited for her label included Nicole Wray, Lil' Mo, and Gina Thompson.

In 2000, Elliott relaunched Goldmind by throwing a party for her new artists. The party's theme recalled the name of her label. Guests were showered with gold confetti, and dancers strutted their stuff in glimmering gold outfits. As she worked the crowd, Elliott hoped the female artists she had signed would help to empower women in the music industry. At the party, she told *Rolling Stone*, "With the Spice Girls, we had the woman power going on . . . hopefully I can bring it back in a serious way . . . A lot of men, like Puffy, throw showcases for their artists, but females need to get out there and do stuff like this. We're just too used to this being a male-dominated field." Elliott was apparently still making sure to promote the

Nicole Wray was introduced to Missy Elliott by one of Elliott's cousins. Wray contributed to the album *Supa Dupa Fly* and signed with Goldmind when she was just 17.

serious message she had laid down in *Da Real World*. She continued to prove that she was not just a music-maker; she was also a woman who wanted to make a difference.

After taking some time to pave the way for others, Missy Elliott felt it was best to get back to her solo career. In 2001, she released her most acclaimed album to date, *Miss E . . . So Addictive*. This time, she and Timbaland had worked hard to create sixteen particularly artistic tracks. Critics were astounded by the results.

"One Minute Man" and "Get Ur Freak On" were the most popular tracks off her third album. She sang more than rapped on "One Minute Man," surprising fans by proving to them that she had a beautiful singing voice. "Get Ur Freak On" showcased original, cutting-edge beats that were also remarkably catchy. In this way, it was a classic Timbaland track. All songs on the album demonstrated Elliott's one-of-a-kind way with words.

Miss E . . . So Addictive was such a hit that, in 2002, it won Elliott several major awards. The Soul Train Music Awards named "Get Ur Freak On" Best R & B/Soul or Rap Music Video. BET dubbed Elliott the Best Female Hip-Hop Artist that year. And, finally, she received her very first Grammy: Best Rap Solo Performance for "Get Ur Freak On." It had been just over ten years since Missy Elliott had left Virginia, and no one could possibly argue that her childhood dream of being a superstar had yet to be fulfilled.

Missy Elliott accepted two Grammy awards in 2002. She won the awards for Best Rap Solo Performance and for Best Pop Collaboration with Vocals, as the producer of the hit single "Lady Marmalade."

CHAPTER FOUR
BEYOND THE MUSIC

The year 2001 was very successful for Missy Elliott. However, it was also tragic. On August 25, Aaliyah was killed in a plane crash while returning home from a music video shoot. Elliott was devastated. Aaliyah was a good friend of hers and was her favorite artist to work with.

As an ever-devoted friend, Elliott made sure to pay Aaliyah the tribute she felt she deserved. The following year, she participated in a musical showcase put on in Aaliyah's honor. Proceeds went to the Step Up Women's Network, an organization dedicated to

strengthening community resources for women and girls.

Working with the Step Up Women's Network inspired her to become more involved in serving her community. As hip-hop's most celebrated female artist and producer, Elliott saw that she had the power to change the world. She decided to put her fame to good use by becoming a spokesperson for Break the Cycle. This organization, which works to prevent domestic violence, especially appealed to her. She didn't want to see others go through the abuse that her mother had endured.

R.I.P. shirts, which feature airbrushed or scanned pictures of deceased loved ones, have become popular in hip-hop culture. Missy Elliott has used these shirts to pay tribute to Aaliyah during her performances.

GIVING BACK

Later, Elliott also became a representative for MAC Cosmetics' Viva Glam campaign. The campaign donated proceeds from certain MAC products to AIDS research. MAC was proud to have Elliott represent Viva Glam. They knew she was a strong, sincere woman who could grab people's attention. Some of the other female stars that followed in her footsteps were Fergie, Pamela Anderson, Christina Aguilera, and Dita Von Teese.

Elliott was also able to use her fame and fortune to give back to her mother, Patricia. She could never forget how strong and supportive her mother had been while she was growing up. She was pleased to be able show Patricia her gratitude by providing for her. "I bought her a 20,000-square-foot house, and three cars. For Mother's Day, being able to give her a check for $100,000, that feels good!" she told *Ebony* magazine's Kevin Chappell.

In 2002, Elliott also chose to take a greater interest in her health. Through diet and exercise, she lost seventy pounds. At first, her fans were upset by the weight loss. They were concerned that Elliott was giving in to pressure from the music industry to be thin. She had to explain to her fans that she had chosen to lose weight in order to strengthen her health, not her image. She wanted to make it clear that she remained a champion of remaining true to oneself.

Her next album, *Under Construction*, was named after the positive changes that she was making in her life. Released in 2002, it had an old-school rap and funk feel. She and Timbaland used samples from artists such as Run-DMC and Frankie Smith to create tracks that reminded them of the early days of hip-hop.

Under Construction's most popular tracks were "Work It" and "Gossip Folks." "Work It" was a catchy single that became one of Elliott's greatest hits. In 2004, it won her another Grammy for Best Female Solo Rap Performance. "Gossip Folks" addressed the current rumors about her, including negative talk surrounding her weight loss. It reminded listeners that even though Elliott was a big star, she was still a person with feelings. *Under Construction* became the best-selling female rap album ever, after selling 2.2 million copies. Missy Elliott had made great history.

Missy Elliott feels her health has improved after losing weight through diet and exercise. In 2007, she teamed up with the show *Extreme Makeover* to award four under-privileged teens scholarships to a weight loss program.

As her already colossal fame continued to grow, television producers again came running to work with her. In 2003, UPN offered Elliott her own reality TV show. It was named *The Road to Stardom with Missy Elliott*. It aired in 2004 and starred a cast of young, aspiring hip-hop artists competing to sign with Goldmind. Elliott served as both a judge and mentor on the show. She hoped the show would help viewers to see the reality of the music world. "I wanted people to see the stages before becoming an artist, like it's a hard grind," she said to Yahoo! Music. The winner of the show was Jessica Betts, who, as of 2008, continues to work on her debut album with Goldmind.

Although Elliott was happy to encourage aspiring artists through *The Road to Stardom*, she opted not to proceed with a second season. The tough competition had given rise to several fights and emotional breakdowns among the contestants. She was not interested in continuing to surround herself with this type of drama. She wanted to make fans happy, not upset! However, she did continue to make television appearances. She became a commercial spokesperson for several big-name products, including Doritos, GAP corduroys, and Vanilla Coke.

In 2004, she signed a deal with Adidas, allowing her the opportunity to create a line of athletic apparel. She named the line Respect M.E. The line, which continues to be sold in stores today, includes clothing, footwear, and accessories. Elliott was excited to collaborate with Adidas because the brand was very popular during the early days of hip-hop.

BACK TO THE MUSIC

After experimenting with television, Elliott felt that it was time to return to music. In 2005, she released an album titled *The Cookbook*. To her fans, the most compelling thing about the album was that it was not entirely produced by Timbaland. This fact caused them to assume that Elliott and Timbaland were in the midst of a disagreement. She insisted that she and Timbaland were still friends. She claimed that she had not enlisted his help on every track simply because she wanted to try something new. The public did not believe her, however, when Timbaland issued the following quote to MTV: "Missy's too over-the-top for this hip-hop. It's a different era, it's not the same. Some of these songs that are out right now [are] songs that I know if we played two, three years ago, people would have laughed at us."

Missy Elliott and Timbaland reunited to work on Elliott's 2008 album *Block Party*, which features singles "Best Best" and "Milk & Cookies."

Hip-hop devotees were in a panic about the presumed feud between Elliott and Timbaland. They felt that the pair's relationship was crucial to hip-hop. In an effort to repair the famous friendship, a group of young fans put together a MySpace page titled "Reunite Timbaland and Missy." The moderators of the group site asked others to join them in signing a petition in order to "Help us let [them] know we're ready for the days when they challenged other producers and artists to step their game up, instead of just bowing down to the mainstream." The page recruited more than 1,500 members. It was apparent that Elliott and Timbaland mattered a great deal to hip-hop listeners.

As Timbaland's greatest friend, Missy Elliott knew that his comment to MTV had not been meant to hurt her. "He was saying it in a good way," she explained to *Rolling Stone*. "Like, I'm so far-left, people might not be ready for me." She went on to assure her audience that she and Timbaland would continue to work together in the future. Elliott's fans trusted her and, therefore, were reassured. Some were even glad that Timbaland had not contributed as much to her latest album. They wanted Elliott to have the chance to prove that her talent did not depend on Timbaland's tracks.

She did prove herself with *The Cookbook*. The album received rave reviews despite Timbaland's absence. "Tim appears on just two of *The Cookbook*'s 16 tracks, [but] the album doesn't lack spice. It's like really good jerk chicken and it's Missy, Missy, Missy that we're feasting on," said *Stylus* magazine.

The Cookbook's first single, "Lose Control," earned her six MTV Video Music Award nominations. Awards were ultimately granted to Elliott in the Best Dance Video and Best Hip-Hop Video categories. "Lose Control" certainly deserved these awards. The track was considered by many to be ingenious. It was based almost entirely on complicated percussion rhythms, rather than melodies. The single went platinum five times, becoming her most popular single to date.

The year after she released *The Cookbook*, Elliott was nominated for five Grammy Awards. She won the award for Best Short Form Music Video for "Lose Control." It was her fourth Grammy.

By 2007, not a soul could deny that Elliott was the most successful female hip-hop artist that had ever been. That year, hip-hop's biggest stars came together to pay tribute to her on VH1's *Hip Hop Honors*. Such guests as Timbaland and Ciara performed a portion of her greatest hits, including "Lose Control" and "The Rain." Her friends enjoyed paying tribute to her contribution to hip-hop. She had encouraged them to be themselves, make creative choices, and stand up for what they believed in. They felt that she was a true musical hero. If only little Melissa singing to her doll babies in her bedroom could have seen whom she was to become!

Elliott had literally gone from rags to riches, so her story is the stuff of superheroes. Perhaps that's why Universal Pictures bought the rights to her life story in 2006. Legendary actor Robert De Niro is producing the movie, which is yet to have a release date. Of course, Missy Elliott's story has only just begun.

TIMELINE

1971 Missy Elliott is born Melissa Annette Elliott in Portsmouth, Virginia.

1992 Hip-hop imprint Swing Mob signs Elliott and her girl group, Sista.

1995 Producer Sean "Puff Daddy" Combs hires Elliott to rap on Gina Thompson's single "The Things You Do."

1996 Elektra Records grants Elliott her own imprint, Goldmind.

1997 Her first solo album, *Supa Dupa Fly*, is released; she receives three MTV Video Music Awards nominations.

1998 Elliott receives two Grammy nominations for her performance in "The Rain."

1999 *Da Real World*, her second album, is released; MTV names the video for "The Rain" one of the one hundred greatest music videos ever made.

2000 *Da Real World* is nominated for a Grammy for Best Rap Album.

2001 *Miss E . . . So Addictive* is released; her friend and collaborator Aaliyah is killed in a plane crash.

2002 Elliott wins her first Grammy: Best Rap Solo Performance for "Get Ur Freak On"; *Under Construction* is released; she wins her second Grammy: Best Female Solo Rap Performance for "Scream, a.k.a. Itchin'."

2004 "Work It" wins Elliott yet another Grammy for Best Female Solo Rap Performance; she and Adidas launch the clothing line Respect M.E.; BET names her Female Hip-Hop Artist of the Year.

2005 *The Cookbook* is released; the single "Lose Control" wins two MTV Video Music Awards.

2006 Elliott's "Lose Control" video wins the Grammy for Best Music Video, Short Form; *Respect M.E.* is released.

2007 Elliott is honored on VH1's *Hip Hop Honors*.

DISCOGRAPHY

1997	*Supa Dupa Fly* (East/West Records)
1999	*Da Real World* (Elektra/Wea)
2001	*Miss E . . . So Addictive* (Elektra/Wea)
2002	*Under Construction* (Elektra/Wea)
2003	*This Is Not a Test!* (Elektra/Wea)
2005	*The Cookbook* (Atlantic/Wea)
2006	*Respect M.E.* (Goldmind/Atlantic)

GLOSSARY

album A collection of songs, usually contained on a record or compact disc.

ballad A story told in a song.

break A section of a song during which there is a break from the main vocals, tune, and beat.

CEO A chief executive officer, or highest-ranking officer, of a corporation.

cutthroat Competitive.

funk A highly danceable form of R & B music, created through emphasizing the beat instead of the melody.

hip-hop producer The creator of the instrumental portion of a hip-hop track.

imprint A brand name.

lip-sync The act of moving one's lips to a prerecorded sound.

mainstream The majority of the population.

MC A rapper.

mixing The act of electronically mixing two tracks together.

music industry The business of music.

percussion instrument Any object that can be hit, rubbed, scratched, kicked, etc., to make a rhythmic sound.

Rastafarian language A language that originates in Jamaica and reflects an African heritage.

remix A new version of an older song created through mixing.

sample A prerecorded portion of a song used in mixing.

scratching The act of creating a musical sound by moving a vinyl record back and forth on a turntable.

soul music A type of music that combines R & B and gospel.

Soul Train A long-running television program dedicated to R & B, soul, and hip-hop.

FOR MORE INFORMATION

Atlantic Records
1290 Avenue of the Americas
New York, NY 10104
(212) 707-2000
Web site: http://www.atlanticrecords.com
This record company owns Missy Elliott's Goldmind imprint.

Break the Cycle
5200 W. Century Boulevard, Suite 300
Los Angeles, CA 90045
(310) 286-3383
Web site: http://www.breakthecycle.org
This organization works to prevent domestic violence.

WEB SITES

Due to the changing nature of Internet links, Rosen Publishing has developed an online list of Web sites related to the subject of this book. This site is updated regularly. Please use this link to access the list:

http://www.rosenlinks.com/lhhb/miel

FOR FURTHER READING

Bankston, John. *Missy Elliott*. Hockessin, DE: Mitchell Lane
    Publishers, 2004.

Collins, Tracy Brown. *Missy Elliott*. New York, NY: Chelsea
    House Publishers, 2007.

Lawlor, Michelle. *Missy Elliott*. Broomall, PA: Mason Crest
    Publishers, 2007.

Waters, Rosa. *Hip-Hop: A Short History*. Broomall, PA: Mason
    Crest Publishers, 2007.

BIBLIOGRAPHY

Brunner, Rob. "Missy Elliott." *Entertainment Weekly*, November 2002.

Chappell, Kevin. "Eve and Missy Elliott: Taking RAP to a New Level."
    Ebony, August 2001.

D., Davey. "Missy Elliott Speaks." Davey D's Hip-Hop Corner. 1997.
    Retrieved January 23, 2008 (http://www.daveyd.com/
    missyelliott.html).

Diehl, Matt. "Supa Dupa Fly." *Entertainment Weekly*, 1997. Retrieved
    January 23, 2008 (http://www.ew.com/ew/article/
    0,,288987,00.html).

Ehrlich, Dimitri. "Missy Elliott—Interview." *Interview*, May 2001.

Eliscu, Jenny. "Women Who Rock: Missy Elliott." *Rolling Stone*, October 30, 2003. Retrieved January 23, 2008 (http://www.rollingstone. com/artists/missyelliott/articles/story/5938700/missy_elliott).

Hauser, Evelyn, and Jennifer M. York. "Black Biography: Missy Elliott." Answers.com. 2005. Retrieved February 1, 2008 (http:// www.answers.com/topic/missy-elliott?cat=entertainment).

Intro.de. "Missy Elliott." 2004. Retrieved April 4, 2008 (http://www. intro.de/kuenstler/Missy%20Elliott).

Johnson, Tina. "Seven Questions with Missy Elliott." VH1.com. 2001. Retrieved February 1, 2008 (http://www.vh1.com/artists/ interview/1443778/05162001/elliott_missy.jhtml).

Juzwiak, Rich. "Missy Elliott—*The Cookbook*—Review." Stylus Magazine.com. 2005. Retrieved March 29, 2008 (http://www.stylusmagazine.com/reviews/missy-elliott/ the-cookbook.htm.)

Kenyatta, Kelly. *Aaliyah: An R & B Princess in Words and Pictures.* Phoenix, AZ: Busta Books, 2002.

Mumbi Moody, Nekesa. "Elliott Offers More Conventional Formula." Yahoo! Music. 2005. Retrieved April 2, 2008 (http://music. yahoo.com/read/news/21240488).

Musto, Michael. "Missy Elliott—Interview." *Interview*, June 1999.

Prezant, Joshua. "Missy Elliott: The Countdown." *Rolling Stone*, 2007. Retrieved March 29, 2008 (http://www.rollingstone.com/photos/ gallery/16296997/fall_music_preview_2007_bruce_spr/photo/ 27/large).

VH1.com. "Hip-Hop Honors 2007: With Honors—Missy Elliott." October 8, 2007. Retrieved March 29, 2008 (http://www. vh1.com/video/play.jhmtl?id=15700318vid=177681).

Vineyard, Jennifer. "Missy Relaunches Goldmind Label." *Rolling Stone*, June 2000.

INDEX

ABOUT THE AUTHOR

Bethany Bezdecheck writes on a variety of nonfiction topics for teens and is a genuine Missy Elliott fan. She lives in New Jersey with her husband and their dog, Maximus.

PHOTO CREDITS

Designer: Thomas Forget; Editor: Bethany Bryan
Photo Researcher: Cindy Reiman